T0326271

PASTORAL

CAMBRIDGE
UNIVERSITY PRESS

University Printing House, Cambridge CB2 8BS, United Kingdom

Cambridge University Press is part of the University of Cambridge.

It furthers the University's mission by disseminating knowledge in the pursuit of education, learning and research at the highest international levels of excellence.

www.cambridge.org
Information on this title: www.cambridge.org/9781316606780

© Cambridge University Press 1942

First published 1942
First paperback edition 2016

A catalogue record for this publication is available from the British Library

ISBN 978-1-316-60678-0 Paperback

PASTORAL

by

JAMES TURNER

CAMBRIDGE
AT THE UNIVERSITY PRESS
1942

CONTENTS

SUMMER

Experience and the lonely hours of pain!
Those absolute hours, formless, without image,
tenor, shape,
gargantuan spaces like enough to death!

Body is a vessel voyaging seas uncharted,
haunting dark paths unmapped to lands unseen,
adventures rare and figures wonderful and strange,
Mandeville or Odoric or Martinez
who found the city of Manoa
and the emperor's guests
scented with powdered gold,
or Raleigh and the good Tivitivas;
spiral infinities infinite tramroutes.
Unheralded journey with unending road!
Spin the long heated chain and grasp
the pole of burning sapphire!
Depths of eternal loneliness!
Dissolution
into Self in pain's long lapsing walk
on tiny skeleton stilts.
O to be free, to loose the gin of pain,
to bite away the foot caught in the snare,
to lose this body but to gain a world,
to run forever from the smell of pain!

(5)

Summer is icumen in with
diversity of experience
casting this reality of passion and hatred
into the cup of life.

Squadrons in echelon braved the clouds.
One looked from a window up to unaccustomed sky
towards the drone,
he beheld there the face of death.
Fear took the heart, remembrance
came to add its sorrow.
Frailty of man born to this day!
Wailing through the hollow land,
(by the waters of Babylon we sat down)
fear and a look behind the back,
and longing to grasp the familiar thing,
to avoid terror in another's eyes,
to plant the feet deep in old earth
and to look with trebled intensity
of vision into the blue,
into the heart of heaven.
Draw forth its secrets and repose!

Summer is icumen in with
day in wonder and a summer sky
cleared for death. Death will pass us by,
murmur of death touches us.
In the valley is life.
Yet there in the blue is life
and longing and misunderstanding.

Nature stands apart, aware and coiling on herself.
Can man alone tread out this press of hate?
In the street men poured blue tar.
Crevices for ants!

Earth stood in silence at the fear
unleashed, spread, menaced, tearing
in pieces the thin veil of reality.
This, at last, was naked truth
for which, O God, we've hungered down the years.
Sunflowers were opening in the garden.
In Oxford, too, the lilac, the laburnum
died to seed.
Summer dust hung in trees, in the silence,
in the fear.
Sea moaned to the rising crescendo of noise
and battle came as moving leviathan
with unthoughtfor speediness.

Remembrance replaced the lace of reality
awaiting deadly night and the sky laminated
by eager searchlights.
But never, then, silence.
Only a hush as when familiar cricket
ceases to chirrup under the oaken beam
of the sunparlour.

Curtain of nights falls over the amber sea
where the inflamed sun engraved its colours.
We, in the land, prepare for night.
Dark hands of sleep spin an ageless fantasy of dreams,

and Time and Memory once were bordered by the
cooling streams
of Lethe and all forgetfulness.

Now, night segmented by the endless drum
of spinning wheels and cogent machinery,
night split by horror, sky
vibrant and alive with nameless fear.
Dark embers of sun have grayly burnt.

At night I have walked the streets of the city,
or seen, moon-given-back in running brooks,
the image of her love,
or woven dreams over the beauty of her fair body
like a flower opening at sunset.
Tall factories with their dirty glass windows
have shone our image into her eyes.
But the streets, then, the accustomed blocks
were still, clean and part of life;
the pools verdurous, mantled by falling night
where grasshopper croaked his solitary song.

The dead stand behind us in shadowy groups.
By night the tall factories are a heap of ruins,
and pools reflect the obscene wings of death.
Above, the moon eats the clouds
and the enemy continues his pathetic voyage
in space, in fear, in unconscious agony.

We, in the land, look backwards
to that gray group, so early come to watch
our crazed mortality,

so recently our loved and true companions,
so once, so soon our lovers.
Now, swaying in grief they pass silently,
their eyes awakened and remote.
To think that this was theirs, that this,
the country of the blind was ours as well!
Sad dim groups whose last permission
was the sad sweet pain of death!

We have loved the nights, frail clouds clustered to the moon,
the silent hours, the lonely woods
and trackless meadows.
Gone to the fields of blood and death!
A turtle-dove spreads its fantail into the spinney,
owl gives its last dismal dawn call,
(is there hope and wonder, is there wonder?)
and the glade is sunshot with purple light.
Dawn has broken the still clouds of night,
there is orange and the blue in long streaks
over the horizon.

A shrew pierces the litter of leaves
with needle-bright eyes.
With spray of kingfisher over the garden pool
world is shattered into life.

Blue poppy is a young girl
in innocence. Clear water-streams
fall over the bright pebble-bed,
and on high hills
snow blackens the cloud-curtain.

(9)

Blue poppy in wistful loveliness
breaks open the secret of day.

Her long slender fingers dip into the bowl of dew,
her feet spread out the flowers of scarlet pimpernel,
her round honeycoloured breasts caress the rose-petals
of apple blossom,
and her hair is the tendrils of the young vine.

Shyly the fawn floats down the springy glade;
there is no noise but the antiphon of birdsong.
No fear in the eyes so liquid and so near to tears.
Her muscles lift her flesh-pale thighs
over summer turf.
She has come to welcome the sun,
her arms uplifted and her hair touching her waist.
She is dance and light of dawn sun,
dance of pipes
under early morning.

O my earth that is a heaven of delight!
Fruits hang in clusters secretly intertwining
their green heaviness with drooping leaves,
gold of sunflower seeds are yet to be
empollened by the hungry bee, going laden
to the hive with her ton of honey.
Snail bears its weight between rows
of rain-fattened onions, green the stalks
of their upthrust growth. Only the haulm
of the potato trails languidly
over brown earth.

The bee encumbered now with myriad pollen

falls into the sweet syrup of its longing
and is immortal.

Toad with opal eyes breathes into lush grass
a long, daylong sigh. At terrible speed,
from world to world, the graceful grasshopper
makes his exploratory bound. Dust hides
the ever present sting of the father nettle
with his pure dress of virgin white.
There sings the cuckoo in his chiming
tiresome duotone.
O melancholy bird!

Elm tree painted on this summer screen
beside the swelling oak holds within itself
some centuries of natural life observed.
It has known winds and troughs of calm,
owl, acorn and the shrivelled leaf,
the boxkite of last century's school children,
and now the deadliest bird of all,
the bomber,
and barns
sketched into the picture
in light brown shirts and hats of country dun.

Where the whitethroat has nested
it is spring. Unseen in the cool
she made her yellow nest.
Among tall nettles with their white cupflowers
she is hidden and quiet.
In scented night she will brood there
beneath moonstreaks. She will awaken

to morning wind along tall elms,
and see the fall of apple blossom.
Where the whitethroat has nested
it is spring.

Thus are there regrets
even now though it is high summer
and going to the dog days
with the rising of Sirius.
There are regrets.

Clustered about the hive the bees
are coming to the end of their honey flow.
Flowers are no longer so sweet since
they have been so variously visited.
In high summer when the grasses
were dying into straws,
I found the nest of the whitethroat
deserted and left with its last
tender farewell and reminder—one egg
unhatched!
Melancholy of age and ave of death,
one pale egg now first discovered!

Grasses fall like books off a shelf
before the blade of the scythe.
Old Time had come to bring his legacy of yellow leaf.
In the orchard apples took sun into their juices.
Old Time swept now about the trees
to open up the paths, unleaf the fruit
and to discover this simple reminder
of spring.

The whitethroat has gone to its lonely fate,
the leaf will fall in a handful of weeks,
tall elms will brace themselves to rushing wind,
the drone will come to meet his unlamented death,
and Time will be a deadened weight
of glistening pearls.

Rainbow reflected in shot silk,
vermilion and cerise of garden flowers,
the scented red of roses!
Tall luminous larkspur in colours unrealizable,
untouchable and pure!
The summer spider lost within the house
making its way across the carpet,
and the fly which touches all and with the bee
knows all experience of flight,
who knows the dungweed as she knows the rose
and battens joyfully on rotten meat,
as she with eager love attempts the sweets
of antirrhinums and the jack bloom of the marrow,
or caught in honied dreams will visit
dark clover, mignonette, the viper's bugloss
and pink campion.
The foxtail grasses bowed with feather seed
await the wind,
mirrored in thunder pools
beside the path.

Life shows its glory. Earth can never exhaust
the wonder of its colours.
Summer dying into autumn's mists

creates a yellow world where carrot leaves
are tinted red and that great bee
resounds its colours in the fruits.
Sunflower lowers its ample head
to take the bees, the hoverflies and ants,
weighting it with a swarm,
its pollen gold like some Egyptian tomb
where Tutankhamen lay
alone and undisturbed
and free from all decay.
And mists enshroud the early morning sun,
the empty roads with fairy oberon-magic
and the spider's jewelled veil.

The earth stands still.
Nightjar has croaked its moonlight song, but in the valley
a lark still sings;
though night has battened down the hatches
of this ever old and ever new old world,
the lark will sing its way
into the song of nightingale.
In the valley shadows are long fingers
formed by the moon from trees and hills.

She is the wonder of that ashen world,
the pale smooth echo of that other light.
She is calmness of a ceaseless time
when earth grows old and weary in the bones,
staying its journey complexed by the sun.
She is the silent gleam
revolving on the well-oiled grooves of age,

the tender, soothing fingers of dark night,
too, too revealing, lucid and too kind.
She soothes to sleep the weary piteous world,
she paints her earth a deeper shade of green,
a lighter black, a less than brazen gold.
She is the wonder of an earth at rest.

So summer ends. We move to periods
of calm days and velvet hours.
Earth has swollen its blossoms.

If I had loved in vain she knew my love.
If we have parted there is all death
in which to love again. Grave cannot be cold
for we must love.
Can she forget the marsh birds calling by the dyke,
churches with ivy-covered walls and barns
aged with lichen?
Things of the past,
memories in poetry, not based on life!
But they were part of life since life
is not foursquare nor round but tenuous,
fleeting, wraithlike, sometimes known.
This summer, grimed by death's sooty hand,
they formed the picture, formed the moods,
they were the emotion, impetus and joy
of what was left of life so almost now
the yawning grave,
the hollow tomb
and pitiful last home.

O gentle orchard, where moths at twilight
linger over dying blossom. Where
songthrush morsels the too-daring worm,
and where the silver whitethroat comes
to spy her pregnant branch.
Spines of the hogweed brittled and snapped,
lay derelict like slender pipes of an organ.
Shadows upheld life in aspects of alarm,
the air was a deep threat and in grass
a lonely doom.

Sun set in the elms orange, blue,
a wound in the sky pouring blood.
World had ended in trough
of sunset.
Secret night beat out its drums
under burnished sky.
Elms
and the orchard apples faded into the dark.
Missel thrush, nearer the house,
brooded, for her token, in the branchcrook,
her cedar home a finger's space from civilization.
She came for comfort and she found a home.
Into the hidden trees snapped the bat,
and stillness fell from burnishment of day
to deep pools of darkness.

In this moment of fear I had come home.

AUTUMN

Summer's last trumpet-blast has ripped the awning
of its gay pavilions.
Wind the horn over lonely hills
to echo across black tarns
and through untenanted crevasses where grow
the unseen ferns,
that shepherd now may know
the wistful days
and autumn's trees
agleam
with gold of ancient helmets.
So falls the yellow leaf,
symbol of dust, the grave and death's
old feast.

We celebrate the year.
Bright seasons
have languished to the yellow candlelight
of autumn. In the still undertone is
heard the death of all, echoing new life.
The old leaf falls to show closed
bud buoyed already in the gale
on whipping branch.
We recollect the year
and carry it with praise down to the vaults,

to shut the door over its golden tomb.
Bare earth of downland rolls to the river,
and plough boulders soil into Time's
long series of furrows.
Nothing is lost;
all in one moment is fulfilled. Only
the future, dim spring along the woods,
only the past, a summer dusty in the lanes,
a purple emperor alighting on the petals
of a michaelmas daisy, is left this side of death.
The trap has dropped.
Nature has shut her thaumaturgical door.

Tractors with iron teeth have milled across
the acres, making the land
a wilderness of seeded nettle,
hogweed, dock and couch.
Yet Earth is bare.

In this intensity of vision earth
becomes at last the Earth
to be loved and looked at,
held within the hand and loved,
moulded by cold fingers, dropped in powdery dust,
dragged up by heavy feet;
a thing suddenly sought for in excess
of sentiment, as God or lover,
mistress or divine courtesan.

Farewell sweet summer and the long day's toil!
Farewell the lazy evening hours
and midnight talk under the limes!

Now Fear makes merry.
Fear this great leveller!
Autumn cringes away into the earth,
away, reality without reality.
A blaze of lights, the sudden explosion,
the cry for help and the falling
sickness of the stomach are the portion
of this coloured season.
Over night air wails the siren
into quiet barns, into mean backyards,
across the fields to mansion salon
and to cottage trim.

Beauty shares the skies with Death!

Gnat-like the spectre floats in the empyrean,
peregrine with white fantail!
Afternoon wind brings sea-breath
through macrocarpas, through the knotted rye-grass.
Floats overhead that beauty split with fear,
spanning the sky, in imagination, from pole to pole.

The tiger may roar in the jungle!

With speed of light out of the sun,
out of that blazing arc, infinitesimal opponents approach,
and in our eyes and the eyes of our companions
the battle is joined.
Mail-clad champions of past tournaments,
atoms of power selfless and impersonal!
Some impersonal battle of dinosaurs,
diminished down the crumbling stairway of Time,
sketched on the backsheet of communal stage.

2-2

Beauty remains.
Artistry does not fail
as the ghost of death dives vertically,
alternates its course, sparing its destiny,
suddenly,
by its own incomparable, invisible power.
Dives away, particle of incredible beauty,
from those now powerless enemies,
and southward joins itself, as if in communion,
to the sun.

What have they to do with us?
Or we, rooted in this mother earth
to whom death is, as life, a simple necessity,
with them?

Peregrine has gone
splitting Time with its second's departure.
Hawks, humming to their hives,
leave nothing but a clear pool of gold-shot blue,
blue as the outer garment of the Madonna.

I stood then at the window. Here
was the end.
My love came to me from autumn shadows,
her offering the sieve of memory
from the oriel window of night-folded sea,
my love with all tenderness!
I see her eyes sad and forlorn,
I see her hands weary with endless beseeching.
But, in the shadows, truth is no longer
a shadow.

Truth is the widowed mother, slaughtered
children scattered in the streets,
filthy shelters and the falling wall,
burning labyrinths of old men's houses,
and firemen pitched like chaff
into the cold-hot arena;
the shattering ram of bomb, the headless corpse,
the muck of flesh and rubble,
and wail of siren in the night.

I would not leave the rotting earth
unseen, unfelt, unknown.
Here is the truth.
Why flee the strife Nature makes known?
The double axis of this polar life
we only see but do not grasp.
Make life a garden of the fairest flowers
then life is dull and languid,
dead and gone.
Adder grins its dread into the bird,
tiger will spring to have its daily food,
and underneath a stone
must always be those lesser wonders
that will fright a child.
I would not have my hope dulled or obscured,
then must I fear.
I seem to see the sunrise come again
in autumn's sheen and polish;
then must I see the maggot in the rose,
the wireworm in the stem, the drone's

sad fate, the cat
with weeping rabbit and the fox
come bloodily from roost.

Wind howls over the land deeply
within the woods where colour has been held
in short months.
I would touch all this colour of the world.
The deep red hawthorn hips,
the yellow leaf, soft to the fingers,
the ripening apple with its drowsy wasp,
the swollen pear, the marrow gross and green.
Reach up my arms
and take the tinted leaf,
the lichen and the creeper.
Reach up my arms to catch the falling star,
to grasp the raindrops or to hold the wind.
Or stand a silent lover in this calm.
My mistress now that band of morning mauve
with gold and silver tresses interwoven.

From rising sun to sapless grass my love,
my life and colour of my life.

Long dead the hours of long twilight;
swiftly sun dives behind the trees
and white wood of the glasshouses is pinked.
There is a chill
round the corner and the owl hops
upon the chimney.
In the orchard
black seed-pods of purple vetch

rattle tiny bones and spear-grass
withdraws its sap.
Dance gulls over the plough
and robin calls from telegraph wire.
In these days the sky was split
and, my love, your arms were a retreat.
Must this love, O gay dancing love
of the hills, the glens where we were young,
die on the point of speeding bullet
or bursting bomb?
I will raise my hands and cry
for one short hour to gather up my loves.
Alas, there is none but our meagre selves
drawn into closer fellowship.
This autumn
binds us in experience, in love, in sorrow.
All we have loved, the rilling brook,
the bittern by the bog, the clock at Charing Cross,
a Schubert sonatina, all we have loved,
and who can tell the count?
must live if we must die.
There is no more hope but death and courage,
courage, once more, to take the earth between
the fingers and to mould
destiny with a spade.

There is a calmness in the sun,
a gentle heat at noon dying to chill,
a lovely lingering breath of summer
perfected in dying foliage,

trees unmoved and track
of ants across the ashpath.
Dew drinkable on grass,
on daisies and on leaves.
Now swollen marrows hide their greenness
underneath gold scaly shields
and there is breathed a sigh to make
the sweetness die upon the mouth,
a sigh to what is gone
what is to come.

Life in these hours had wild intensity of Truth,
when all could be or be not in the space
of seconds split.
Infinity walked at the shoulder;
yet the finite was composed loveliness.
Now, this peak of time, now let me grasp
the beauty soon to be denied.

Lowliest flower or insect had wonder
disregarded in a world at peace.
They were the common things;
such magic unperceived,
such pity!
Colours were of infinite depth,
and there was unity.
Collect openly and with speed
all that might have been,
so not a drop be lost.
There is no time to rue the past.
The thousand petals

of the daisy held essence of the glory
fast fading in the holocaust.

In the cataclysm there is no companion.
Across the years she will come to me
through regalia of death
and flux of history.
O my love, I stoop to earth to love thee,
O my tender love be with me now
in loneliness of heart and sickening fear.
Lift up your eyes and you shall see
above the grinning face of death,
birth and its glory
in the autumn leaf,
the well-known streets,
moon balanced on a star,
and berries red in hedges
with the hips.
There is a glory to be seen and held
for one brief moment,
one moment greater than a million years,
for with this fear the eyes can see, heart
may communicate its lonely pain.

Who now will open earth's sweet secret store
or search her closet for a tiny seed
or come to watch the sun gold-up the moor,
to see the dabchick in its bed of reed?

Earth from her hands drops down a thousand joys
and pleasures rich and rare.

Luxurious earth with claws reddened with blood,
with luxuries, with wealth secretly hid.
Gold falls to earth.
Her hands will pour
the stream of molten metal,
until gray cold with chilly fingers come
to ice this potent flame, to kill the sap,
to rot the bindweed where it choked the rose,
to crack the water and to build
in pyramids its shining crystal wall.
Worlds have no meaning to this force of earth,
she laughs at wealth, kills without sin,
murders her lovely ones, creation's pride
she bears away to one cold loathsome grave.
And all is gone beneath her icy shroud
till miracle of earth will come again.
She cares not men shall slaughter from her skies,
that children skip she cares not, that they bleed
she puts no meaning to.
What cares she
that a child shall weep and die,
who has seen death a million million years,
who has seen life in all its fairness spring
beneath the touching midwife of her hands?
The strong shall sicken into weakness,
the fair grow ugly while she laughs
within the portals of her secret home
remote.
Her rule is death, sweet cloying death,
or rabbit bleeding from a ferret's tooth,

or rust and mildew up a flower's stem.
Her portion leaves her ugliest, she
loves her too compelling beauty with a lust
making her kill.
The fawn will die to deck her funeral chest,
the goldfinch hover to her shroud,
still autumn's shroud of purple, gold and red,
and crimson blood and corpses stiff
with winter. So she does, all-seeing
and all-rich.
She can afford her murders,
laugh at sin, since only man
created knows her not.

Where were I without my companions in this
lonely journey?
And with them to observe this my Becoming
what have I to do?
Am I come without purpose, lonely and obscure,
a joke of Nature's, nay, her greatest jest?
Without them all the roses in the world
were nothing but a mass of coloured matter,
with perfume none since none could know
their smell or even that they were.
In vain the butterfly would hang upon the leaf,
and day would break upon my heart
with knell of an eternal doom.
From Being, then, from that primaeval Sleep,
we pass to magical Becoming,
to strife of living

and the hates and loves,
yet now alone with knowledge of our
loneliness and sorrow.
Did Nature in her vasty conversations
with energy, her other self,
spue me from ancient bogs where
grow the lianas seen by none,
deep in their penetralium,
a green, unwakened, loveless, mystery world,
moving forever from the flower to seed,
from seed to flower again?
Me did she dower with the gift
of thought and consciousness
for reason only to herself now known?
Yet without me who then could see her come
unfolding touchingly her wondrous weeds
to give again the sun its lordly place?
The sun boils there.
Its flaming jets bite to the depths of night,
a long burnt ember of the dawn.
Must she make me to live and live alone,
and then to die back to her earth,
and then for her to laugh like Zeus
shaking Heaven when he played the god
with silly mortals?

The dark tower stands by the sea
buttressed by rock.
O my love, do you remember
the wheeling sea-birds and the empty shore,

the basalt rocks, the birdless sea
and pools mirrored within themselves
where grew mauve seaweed with its
tangled hair, where glowed strange lights
and where, under level water, pebbles
glistened to white, to gold and yellow, to red,
to blue? The little shells, the boulders
and the yawning gulfs?
The dark tower stands with its halo
of white birds. Overhead spins the sun,
moon and lostness of Space.
I will take you to my arms again
and whisper,
Love is enough for all this hate,
this misery and death, for all,
Love is enough.
And Space
can go with Time into
the den of old philosophers to make them weep
at the beauty of its unexplainable
and mathematical exactitude.
Who loves has Space,
has Time, has God and all eternity.
His heart swings with the universe,
and systems made
and systems broken fall through his hands,
chaff from the corn.

The hare knows stillness of dawn,
her eyes move, her body upright

feels yet the rising warmth of her
not deserted form.
Red streak is a jagged saw
across the body of night,
reflected secretly
in untroubled waters of deep-hidden country pools,
where stands the heron
to acclaim the day.
Brass candlestick of moon divides
geometrically night sky and earth,
calmly swings away towards the bowl of day,
swings over earth in everlasting nostalgia.
Come, now, to see the reed beds
wrapped in the dawn, the bittern standing
in the flags,
the brilliant moss-green garment
for the fallen tree,
the long-drawn sigh of waking world.

Shadows in black fingers striated the lawn,
a globe of yellow reflected the open window.
Within the room was a haunting of ghosts,
speechless quiet and red pattern of the carpet.
Marsh was present in the air.
Many the long cones formed on trees
rattling together, twisting skeletons,
skulls laughing at dullness
of this seeming reality.
Her eyes saw only the yellowed lawn,
and she heard the sudden call of the curlew,

the awakened bleat of sheep,
the haunting bell of the church clock.
O my love can you see nothing else
but day we shall no longer love,
day when we shall be ghosts to one another
as the shades here in this room?

And so I rode away across the fields
where so lately stood the waving corn
and green blades of barley.
So summer passed to autumn;
the sun had set.
O my love this is farewell,
farewell across the years!
I see you standing by the casement in that upper room,
I see your crimson dress, your hair
moved in the breeze, the sun
a minute dead to me
bears its emblazoning across the dome.
Shield of dying day!
This is my grave.

The silver harness of the horse
shakes and spangles its tiny song,
faded notes of children's music-box.
Was there sadness comparable to this,
that I must go?
The river runs its course.
I must ride on
to the ends of the world
companionless.

In dying day with the tremulous
magic of night, I turn back to thee.
Horse spurs its inexorable feet
to the wood. I see thee still
my love,
O my love.

The falling tear of parting is caught and turned,
forever lost. Ours is but added, burned
in the ashes of all past loves.

WINTER

Wind whistles in hollow trees,
    spears a phantom to the woods,
a stranger without name in decaying lanes,
and on hills the dark shadow
of a pale walker.
Grass saws away to the west as
east wind mows into earth
turning friable soil to solidity.
Over the world howls the deep wind
in a semi-circle, flying to the sky
to sweep clouds off the sun,
lichen off barns
and feathers off the owl.
Cold nature dies within her winter shield,
withdrawing to herself.
She has wept and is still.
She is palled with white, with black
of deadening frost,
with long pencils of stinging rain.

O God the earth is cold, cold and hard
with a dour satisfaction of its grim
intractability.
Where is there warmth?
O God

the earth is cold!
From hour to dusklight hour under
shadeless sun I will bear down upon the earth,
grind its stubbornness into
a straight border.
The earth is cold and lost;
none will come
to succour this utter chill.
Drop down, my heart, into this elemental cold.
This is her portion. Therefore make one
with Nature and deny her not.
Men have travailed in a colder cold.
This is the land of Bede and Becket!
Must we then throw our birthright to the winds
and lie pacifically before the storm,
or throw the heritage of centuries
out on the ash-heap?
I will make cause with all the common men who fight,
that fairness of the earth shall perish not.
I hold that in my hands.
Let others say who see a brighter day,
that men with hearts stood boldly
against the chill of cruel winter
and this continental frost.
Make me a shield to wear my heart upon;
down with the mind when all my heart
cries out for action,
cries out to stand with martyrs,
cries out to take a sword and smite
the hordes of evil

and the well-organized blood-lust.
I cannot nor I will deny the heritage
that makes me man.
I cannot rest with saints while
innocent men and women
are butchered, buried, burned and tortured.
But there shall come an end when
these poor bones shall step
along the Rue de la Paix,
shall peer (with eyeless sockets)
into Versailles Hall and sit unheeding
by memorials.

Gold leaf of the limes has fallen
to the dry bed of the stream.
Lady of Shalott has passed away.
Over meadows sang lonely curlews,
over meadows sounded tiny bells.
O last of the year comes down the leafless woods
with cold on hips
with ice on haws.
Horse pulls afield the shining plough
under dragging clouds, under
weak sun, into the bottom
by the stream where fieldfare sang,
into the ridge of memories.
Lady of Shalott has passed away
with her canopy bright,
her golden jewels and her hair so red.
Deeply into the earth draws the cold,

(35)

cold into static earth,
where stands the eternal magic
where sleeps the magical vision
where fingers delve to warmth.

A time for feathers or for
iron bars.
Body leans to the cold. Wind
dowers the world, scything where plough
has folded the soil. Shining blades
of the blue instrument fall comfortably
into the furrows, two-bladed the lovely
silver collars pulled over the field,
over the old old earth of England,
turning up shards of ancient
pottery, iron bits of crucibles
made in their dawn of life, coins
with strange heads of bold emperors,
and beautiful vases which
were handled by poets and by lovers.
The world is old
but courage is bright, the terrible
thing it was in all history.
Courage against the cold, against blood.

In the ruins she stood exalted,
her hands beseeching in unconscious
supplication, her eyes brave
with sight of hidden mysteries.
In the ruin
is the hand of God made

with tireless energies of creation,
boldly destroying the good and every one
of his own works
save love and courage.
In a moment, time-shattered by the bombfall,
she has seen the universe
turn swiftly on its axis. She has been
a sister to her brothers,
a Spartan among Spartans.
She is the creation of this latter-day
courage. Salute her!

There is cold in barns and down
the stream, cold in sheds
and through the yards.
Cold, cold, numbing cold. Spades
and forks redhot with cold, steel
searing flesh.
Dig, dig
into the earth that
sweetness of fruit may come forth.
Down in the marshes dip the peewits
to the dykes, up over the bean rick.
Nothing but cold
and great bastions of bare trees.
Earth is hard as surfaced road,
no wind can whip it into softness.

In the dogdays we had made the shelter
deep in the boiler pit, with long black
sleepers and bags of sand over.

Now streets are empty in the hush.
Noise of siren has cleared the roads,
noise of siren running down,
uncoiling its hideous welcome as one
unwinds a roll of wire.
Space has emptied of its hurrying atoms
and life lingers on a pinpoint.
No-one enters the street. Sombre, gray,
shadowless it lies deserted as
hollow wind dies wailing over sea.
No dog sniffs up its daily smells.

A cat trips down the ashpath, alarmed
at night-quiet in daytime.
Hush is the hush before an eclipse.
Men and women stand in their houses,
or without word,
accustomed, disciplined,
drop into the shelter, ants
to anthill, for protection.
Trees sway in the breeze and
defenceless houses are daubed against
sky. Paintings on the scene
in a theatre!
Before the face of the black boiler,
in darkness doubled by the slits of light,
in chinks and cracks, sit or stand
the people in their unknown fear.
Hush is as the silence
when Joshua made the sun to be still

and the mountains looked into the sea
and the fishes stopped in the water
and the maid gazed into the mirror
and the horse flung up its harness
to breathe in the air of doom,
the sudden chill of impending death.
World has joined all its pieces
together, the jigsaw is complete
here on the table. So clearly does
the eye see the yellow of the last
chrysanthemum, brown sprigs of cones,
and the earth
black with shade
of approaching horror.

Burning oblation of a bloody sacrifice!
And this for Liberty!
Burns earth,
scarred face of earth, ash-blackened and obscure.
Pile after pile of dead! In the knacker's yard
rats are flung into heaps.
O humanity
O fair body of men
O lovely features without blemish
O strength and glory of white bodies
to come to this!
What eternal pity!
How miserable the death in the snow!
How glorious the mountains of dead
who died that the invader

might not conquer!
There are fair children in the meadows
and lovers.
Now
nothing but charred ashes
of bone, the useless rifle in a frozen ditch,
the rags of uniform and hollow eyes
which once had moments of fair wonder.
Nature has gibbeted her fair ones
on the gridiron where she roasted
St Lawrence. And they have loved
when yellow daisies held the sun
and wind on stream was
hope and proud life.
And this for Liberty!
Graves more fitting than a churchyard,
these funeral pyres are pyres of honour,
the mighty boneyard of grinning Nature
requiring numbers for her mausoleum,
combing her hair in her subterranean cavern,
fetching her ice glass to behold her face
winsome in times to come,
but to-day,
a witch with blackened teeth and shrunken cheeks.
O fair flower of earth,
stand that all may not fall!
Deck these multitudinous heaps,
burnt in the blood of innocent mankind, with
roses white and red.
We are the victims, too.

Each drop of blood is drawn from this
blood brotherhood. The German and the Russian!
Now where lies the difference
since a bone's a bone?
Liberty, stand fast,
that all thy sons
may find a common grave with tyranny
and so pass to a common heaven.
The evil is not in the men who die,
they are the brave.

Sea shifted in the rock pools where
red crabs harboured, crabs with great eyes
inspecting watery worlds. One plunge
from the spit, deep, deep to cleaving
waters! Eyes saw the odd marine creatures
and the lustrous wealth of underwater
stones. A thrust through the narrow channel,
limbs aware, awakened to the sudden fright
of a trap; a pull along the oozy,
velvety walls and the body stood in the cavern
and there a palace saw of wondrous height
with magic lights and clusters of white pearls,
and heard the hidden drip of water
on the sand.
A world now made into a universe
where no bird came.
Feet slid into the sand and a maiden sat
over a cavern pool, her hair about her face,
her hands closed to her eyes.

She did not move, she neither called nor spoke
until I touched her foot.
She raised her head and with her hands
parted those seaweed tresses and I knew.
She was sorrow and misery of the world,
seated alone, to weep alone and brood.
She touched me and her eyes were white,
burning to my heart with pity.

I was of the world.

I left her
for the upward climb to hedge the cliff;
I hear her voice still calling in my ears,
'Where'er thou goest I shall stand with thee
at thy shoulder and within thine heart.'

The slippery rock-holds compass my mind,
and the lonely voices echo
that magnitude of
unexplored vastness.
Hung a lantern
and it was the sky.
Sea roared, closing the secret mouth.
Stand
patiently above the floor and all the sounds
of hell come floating up,
and all the sounds of hell
come floating up.

We have circled the world with indestructible bonds,
peeped pugnaciously into the minds of men
to spy out hidden shores, but still

we must admit Nature's administration to be
of the beautiful the most lovely,
that Alexander had more power than all
the world he conquered,
Olympias,
his mother, every magic
denied to-day to all our wonders.
But this is life, too, my love.
There are paths back in the jungle even
to the ordering of sweet cake in a tea shop,
smoking a cigarette after a day's skating.
Such reality as now sweeps the sky
restricts our liberty, makes of us machines
for vengeance, evokes the I remember,
because in one moment the icy fingers
of death may have languishingly
passed.
Who fears death will not pass in the street
or take wings to mutilate his boredom.
Present minutes ground to hours and days
know not boredom,
only thunder of a cruel blinding experience,
tight like a rope about the forehead
and drawn wire fine. Only thunder
and the I remember
of a dying man,
of dying man.

Even in the cold are days to compensate
when tiny bells of ice hang in switchy hedges,

when plough ridges are haloed by frosty mist
crowned with powdered white.
We sit huddled, broody birds, on the
warm pipes of the glasshouse,
silent,
each absorbed in his own world,
waiting signal to go out into the cold,
to drag barrows over the land,
to scatter frozen dung, to pull
green leeks, their leaves clammed with ice,
to keep company with that ghostly bird
the gull, come presently to feed its
hungry maw on ploughturned soil.
She will reward you for the cold.

No orchard now holds blossom
on the boughs, no bird but robin
sings his hunger note.
Silver fork-teeth chatter into grey earth
as, under the red dusk-light, the sun
reflected through glass, each man leans towards
the earth.
In the quiet of ceaseless work
an old rat nibbles a forgotten crust,
and wipes its whiskers with vicious paws.
A cat minces over the lines of empty flower boxes,
heavy with kittens, restless with unseen
weight of promised birth.

Quiet of day-ending
in weariness and clouds ranged in a band

behind the trees.
Muscles pull at the earth
to raise the silver instrument.
Weariness
in the arms and back. An endless fatigue
that will not let go, that creates sharp pictures,
as the blossom of young tomato vines,
the golden edge of galvanized tank turned
westwards, scarlet robin's coat
with dusky hue.
Weariness
pulling the shoulders down into the mould,
fatigue like aching hunger.
And, in weary vision,
deep in the bosom of this aching tiredness,
I see a god perform his wonders
over the frozen field.
A maiden with a smile and supple limbs.
With them a brachet and a noble horse.

They spin their idle hours, their gossamer threads.
A kiss is given, lightly lip to lip;
featherspin their feet,
touching earth with no more trace
than bird.
Or
flying like swift, borne on air,
untired, ceaselessly alive.

Sweat pours down the arms, coldly
excreted from the toiling body.

Here is my mother earth;
sweet Mother guard me now!
My life, my care and now my all.
Shall my hands crumble it to pieces,
my foot stamp thoughtlessly upon it?
Ages past there have been other civilizations,
yet there remains this crumbling element
to give back life,
to shield in death.

We look.
The whole gang notice suddenly
the disappearance of the sun.
A man sighs.
One rolls down his sleeves, another sinks to earth,
a fourth, blinded with sweat, leans there.
Steam rises from the hotwater pipes,
no salamander bright bespeaks these fumes.
But over my shoulder visions seem to fade
with one last look.

I throw down my fork, stand upright,
regard this flesh, consumer of so many daylight hours.
The fields are bare, crusted with frost.
In my fatigue I dreamed.
Now there is good-night.
Homeward!

My birthday was in the days of security,
when hansom cabs roared up the Strand
and it was fashionable to wear fierce whiskers.

To-day, alas, what have I done to pass these
serpent years?
I seem to see the ebb and flow of Time,
to hold the sequined curtain from the stage
of my own brief past years.
At this age Alexander was emperor to the
known world, had come to the borders
of mysterious China, looked and turned back,
as once, when yet a boy, he had sent
horsemen westward at dusk when the sun
hung its image in long cylinders of light,
westward from Thrace to Europe in search
of lands to conquer. In the evening, then,
for him so many years ago, his scouts came back
with messages of lands deserted
and worlds of wilderness.
And Caesar, too,
at age along with me, was scattering
millions to the Roman mob to make
his crossing of that little river Rubicon
a politic success.
Mozart
had lived. But I have now
no worlds to conquer but myself, no
lands to travel in except my soul, no
people to be emperor to except the shades,
hovering in the past, the ghosts
of thirty years.
Yet I have seen the honeysuckle climb the hedge,
the stoat go warily to kill its prey,

the dawn rise fair upon the hill, and felt
the snow and ice, and seen
miracle of Spring.
Alexander, for all his purple robes,
his fiery steeds maned up the wind, for all
his valour, could not see more nor
wonder more that night, without his help,
could wrap the world he ruled.
Indeed that world was fresh when Philip
went from Macedon to take
his Epirote wife.
And now 'tis stale indeed,
though we have power to freshen up its
face, to clear the rubbish piled
and cluttered up since I was born.
We have the power.
It shall be used.
We must have truth of words beside
this present truth of action,
nor gloss from life
courage and sacrifice,
or fling our penny to the beggar there,
or stutter social nothings in comfortable salons.
We need, and we shall have
a break with that past to which
I was born—that past of hansom cabs
and social injustice.
We need and we shall have
new forging of society and acknowledgement
openly

that man
is never a mere instrument.

The last dim tapers of the year are burned,
squeezed out between wet fingers.
Months have wept themselves from the old
with grim associations to the new.
Saviour of Mankind has been,
has gone with presents
brought for little children.
For them His patriarchal beard
has mingled with the snow.
Gulls wheel inland over lonely plough
and, then, with breath of sea,
outward again to where the halcyon nests,
to brother with the cormorant,
to spy the guillemot off Lundy Isle,
and the puffins of Arran.
The last dim tapers of the seasons flag
in holders, candles flicker into grease,
brass snuffer brings its pyramid
of night.
There is an end.
And, with hope, in snowy cloak,
there is beginning,
circle upon circle.

To-day my lady combed her hair.
Sparks lit the darkness.
At dawn
she glimpsed the mirror and she smiled.

With patience now she runs the comb
along her golden hair. Soft rain
tenderly touches the earth.
My lady
has a bright new dress of goodly green
and sandals light as feathers.

Bemoan no more the chill and icy cold.
Winter departs, the curtain falls.
Who knows, Pandora's box
shall be forever shut,
its rusty locks, its bolts and massive hinges
forever closed with ruin and old age.

SPRING

We still must weep though Spring shall come again
to raise the burdens of the saddest year,
we still must weep if eyes will bear
the tears,
if tears there be unshed.
Trumpets of heralds speak from the woods
if we have ears to hear
and any man withdraw out of this vale
of uttermost sorrow.
Joy in the morning if any left to throw
away the cup of sorrow,
filled like crystal with unhappy
shades of man,
sorrow to creep alone into the hands
of quiet and its rest.
No Spring can raise the trembling lip of sadness.
Yet we must live to cast this shroud away.
Let not our tears and agonies
be relegated to the lumber house.
Europe has need of tears.
Though Spring shall come again,
these days when Chaos ruled
the elephantine world,
when Chaos
walked with cruelty and strode

the mind of man like a gigantic
leopard, do not die
in our hearts.

Withal she comes again, uncaring
Spring with tender hands
to clothe the world in jewels,
displaying loveliness.
Awake, my heart, for there is hope,
lift up this cloth of sorrow,
the veil of tears shall be burnt through
with scalding sadness.
O God, we shall lift up our hearts!
See, Spring
has come
with greenness in thickets,
with little bird,
with crocus, tulip
side by side with mist.

O love that touched the roots of life
springing from known things into the glory
of unknown.
Sadness and sorrow filled the joy.
Who has not loved the sad sweet joy of love?
Her rhythm was my movement,
her laughter mine,
her tears
were not for her alone.
In touch, in words, in all our loves
we shared those tears.

I have lived in these empty rooms,
seen them at night with the moon
flaking walls of their old paper,
or cracking the floorboards or winking
into eyes of rat.
A sudden wonder waited
me when I would creep here under
the roof, a wonder of crystalline light,
of ermine canopy abreast the wall.
She had lived here, the rooms
echoed to her voice calling.
Now nothing but the hollow spaces,
sooty ash in fireplaces, heaps
of dust along the dress cupboard which
once, my love, held that velvet gown
after the ball.
Silver fingers will
write on the wall old legends and tales
of mirth.
Loneliness
stirs up a pile of rubbish, drags
back reality into this stupid
dreamland.

We weep no more for death
since long ago he brushed our coats,
made of himself something uglier
than the usual road accident,
pulled at our sleeves
and passed.

Passed and left us with our dead.
We shall not weep, but laugh,
take him by arm along the city streets,
call him familiar, share his dark
jestbook, welcome him as guest,
let him be overlord
and master of the house.

Will ever lilac bloom so purple,
or laburnum
so yellow as in that last sad spring
in Oxford?
When flows the river
with increasing loneliness; and roads
to Banbury, Woodstock and the north
are symbols known of sorrow and of tears?
When Wytham woods have heard
old love-words vain, and the Priory
at Godstow mocks back at me
for all my toil and pain?
In London in the Spring there has been hunger,
pain in the belly, and gnawing pain
in the chest, and long hour's fight
against suffocating death.
But in Yarnton,
village of dreams,
is only sorrow
that she did not love me.

The hill came forth from night, curves of distant

hills formed to the dawn.
There was no light but many lights,
no dawn but all dawns shatter at my feet,
no russet mantle but a globe of gold,
a circle drawn by druids and the saints.
A loveless beauty and a beauty
without love.

Have we progressed, made worthier the Springs
which followed?
Progress, and the fate
of Time's old wings, renewed each minute
and each minute dead, have dragged away
the years since gone, since once
we stopped to pull the frail fritillary,
or watched, in Addison's walk,
a boy cast line into the river.

We, children of death, acclaim the Spring,
unconsummated flowers, the livening seed
brothers our benches, and stench
of work, boredom of long hours
is haloed by the single thrush;
primrose, violet, and plane tree
caracole even in the din.
Jonquil breathes into the air
and Lydian chords lift the soul
over death, over Jordan, over
Crucifixion.
And we, children of death, acclaim life,

the timeless quiet,
the newfound nest.

Clear the paths for us, we will not be denied.
Who have ruled earth so long
can now deny us not,
for Spring is come to heal death's wounds,
to pull the shroud
from off the rotting corpse,
to sing of life,
to sing to us, swaying in untold companions
along the hard road.
For us the sweat, for us the blood,
for us, at last, the Spring.
And we are come with bloody hands
to reap our harvest, to
beat out drums,
that lion now may lie beside
the lamb.
For we, too, would enjoy the quiet.

He our guide
who has known vast deeps
as the hollow of his hand;
dead and born again and dead once more,
who has taken into him the fruits of all evil
and all good before creation,
before nature,
made it his pleasant grazing ground,
and raised up to touch the hand of God.

Secrets of the grave opened before his eyes,
who came here at dead of night.
Corpses were his yearly
companions down the centuries before
Plato lived.
He has wandered the wilderness of
Beersheba and understood
life in death, and in death
esoteric love.
Who has handled experience as his
daily loaf, is timeless
with everlasting seed.
Upon whom the mantle of love
is no longer a hate,
the flight of bird no more
than swinging of his brain.

The horse will take soft earth in its hooves,
and wren will build its mating nests,
its false husband-nests under the straw
of decaying summerhouse.
One morning
will see the quick flight
of martin journeyed home
to familiar eaves;
one morning
see the tender mayfly hatch,
will see the dragonfly hover to doom
within the confines of the garden pool,
will hear

frog croak its mating welcome,
and will know that horse shifts harness
to be away to meadows and the leas.
Primrose gone,
now spring earth's loveliest
blooms to sway before the visitation
of the bees and to perfume soft air
with scents of an old alchemist's shop.

Sweet gentle Spring! Your fields
and hedgerows wild with unclaimed life,
tokens of promise and of beauty
unborn.
Rivers and streams may flow
the faster and with tender song
unweeping and unwept.
We will come out and take the hand,
the fingers offered, exchange with all
the words of joy, make much ado
and crown thee with a hawthorn halo.
Come sing this seedless song and echo
down the vale.
Have we not waited
with aching heart, with weary limbs,
for little flower,
for willow-wren and swallow?

Dead days are gone into the dark place
where the heart sorrows,
keeping its vigil along with heavy tread;
there is a black coverlet over the bed,

and there, in that place,
are tears.
But now,
O come, my love, let us forget the past
in this one present season
when hoar has melted into earth,
and all is made afresh.
For one moment we will not look back
into the past, for there are haunting ghosts
which soon must take us by the throat
and force our eyes to weep,
our hearts to break
with snapping sorrow,
longing unfulfilled.

The weaver of spells is here over the river,
the necromancer
in his green cloak
with silver stars, his pots of magic and his charms
to soften dull winter, to unfreeze
the blackened grime.
Now snake glides easily along the grass,
tree creeper nimbles up the bark
and woodpecker drums his tattoo endlessly.
Children gape at trees. In skipping,
in song, they border magic faeryland,
their eternal inheritance.
Wistfully they glance over the shoulder
of younger sister.
Bury gloom, uneasiness of heart.

Seasons have echoed through the years
to this bright Spring men cannot shatter,
and only Nature blossom out to blowsy summer.
Night tells of Spring.
The nightjar pouches out its throat
to croak with croak with frog,
there is green slime scumming the bogs,
white mist of quickthorn winter.

The thickets still have nightingales to sing
a merry roundel and to suddenly sadden
a listening heart.
Though men sweat, die in their sweat,
though men may cry God for help,
the nightingale shall sing
and woods shall merry ring
with joyful sound.
Earth's feathers now abound
in this most lovely stound.

Goldfinches
scaling in parabola
from thistle up to mountain ash,
spangle long coloured ribbons
against the green hedge;
tapestry of soft gold cloth
with eminent embroidery.
Green flashing to deeper green,
green hedge, white rowan flower
and a crimson spot
caught in the sunstream;

caught in a chalice;
caught on the silver spearhead
the soldier saw at Golgotha.

One single blackbird piping yellow dusk,
its voice shrilling over wet leaves,
rising and falling
to drops of rain on the pond surface,
coloured in minute reflection by preening
kingfishers and grass-snake darting,
a shade of wire,
from osier bed to osier bed!
Cherry hangs white head above the water
of the pool, mirrored in gauze,
a damsel in her wedding garment.
In the silence raindrops fall
green so green to be almost white,
in dusklight tapering to the west.
There is smell of spring in the old garden,
under trees in the coppice
earth is alive with yellow green stems
of curious plants,
and lords and ladies stand uncrimsoned yet
within their shieldy sheaths.
It is a delicate china world to break
at touch, where twilight bird will call
to twilight bird. Sun will tremble
on lip of meadow-cup and gentle
shades walk
up and down grass paths,

and brush the hedges
honoured by the years.

This is my heritage!
The dark swift river in its oozy bed,
mist-obscured marshes where the crow unseen
caws blackly to the hidden sun.
Red robin, quick and speedy, on the gate
turns down its beady eyes.
The strange stag-beetle in his polished coat
of mail, along the path, intent and dutiful,
and the shafts of a corn-reaper
idle on Sunday morning.
Connect this with invisible reality.
Soft lie the water meads beneath
the intolerable bee-like roar of planes.
Sun breaks the veil, the wistful loveliness
of undisturbed river.
River of light!
Spear shafts to touch both the grey wings
of the lazy-flying heron and the turning wingtips
of the heard embattled.

Across the fields the church clock at Bury
moans over the moistured air.
In all chivalry, in courage and with
incomparable skill (man has his mighty hands
to flash that tiny aluminium atom in and out
of the sunpath,) in love, in sorrow,
and in unutterable joy,
battle is made.

Yet will the turtledove its song intone
nearer my ears. Heron and all lesser birds
pursue their course, the burnet moths,
the crested peewits span their lonely heavens,
their circle of infinity endless
and untouching.
Yet will the turtledove
its song intone.
Can I take one and leave the other?
Can I no longer exercise my choice, my right
to choose the mist-filled meads, the gaps
where chalkpits peer, like eyes,
great yellow eyes?
I will lift up my heart and sing
that both are mine.
That landscape
towering through the veil (seemingly some old
castellated town, a town of towers
and ancient deeds of courage)
is mine.

I will lift up my heart and sing,
for in that other shadow (now pierces
the sun in golden mist, shifting
its hollow tubes of light)
is also my life.
In both I hold a part.
I am because in each I am engrained,
they are because I am.

In this silence I am created.

Printed in the United States
By Bookmasters